Chemical Kisses

Trista Evans

BookLeaf Publishing

India | USA | UK

Presentation by *BookLeaf Publishing*

Web: www.bookleafpub.com

E-mail: info@bookleafpub.com

ISBN: 9789357215183

First edition 2022

*Dedicated to my Family, who always
believed in me, and my Friends, who didn't
complain when I sent them random writing
at three in the morning.*

Formaldehyde

Formaldehyde teeth dipped in cherry
Pits of experience, laced with the drugs
That I stole from you back in college.
The taste of air and acid on my tongue
Is nothing compared to the pain you
Left on my left femur bone/ Where
You sat and sank your nails into my
Flesh, praising me for all the sins
I committed in your name/ The blood
I spilled in order to be worthy of
Muttering such a thing/ You ignored
My pleas and pushed me hard, my
Lungs melting like my bright yellow
scars/ Formaldehyde cigarettes and
Lines of white lies/ The pain in
My brain numbing like winter lashed
eyes/ Those college days are long
Gone, lost with my last dose of
Formaldehyde.

Cadaverine

I always thought that those
Bodies I got back in Little Rock
Looked so peaceful and calmin'.
Their small eyes shut, hands thin
And crossed, like those church
Men I shot all the way back in
Redding/ Those men though,
They didn't go easy, no/ I killed
Them slowly and then let them rot
Within their cages of folly/ The red
Seepin' in to those holy pages, the
Gospel never been so lowly/ Those
Ultramarine eyes that preen with such
Deadly sighs/ That case of Cadaverine
Leakin' with fresh flies, larva mixin'
With the stench of the dead, warnin'
All the Good men that there are tears
To be shed/ Got run outta Redding,
Kicked outta town, and now here
I am, with my bone-white crown,
Sippin' on my ol' Cadaverine.

Oxygen

I smother the fire to let
The cold seep in, so I feel
The same outside as I do
within/ Oxygen glazed tears
Dripping down porcelain skin,
Clinking along the hollow
Walls of Godly sin/ Who
Created me? Why? Pry my
Soul out of the sky and
Put me with the trees, who was
I meant to be? And who will
I become? Oxygen glazed
Lips, kissing without rosy
Red tongues.

Peroxide

She tossed her head back,
Downing a glass of dyed
Blue—throat burning and
Teeth worming through
The flesh of her cheeks,
And the tender touch of
The tongue/ Peroxide
Sighs of final dues, acceptance
Of the world and what
She went through/ The
Sting of the glass echoing
In hand/ And the clapping
Of the drunken man, that
Sat and wallowed behind
Her seat, swirling their
Glass of Peroxide dyed
Blue.

Iodine

They say the Gods will walk again.
From their heels bursting low clouds
Of rumbling depth, bubbling will the touch
Of death/ Iodine saliva of forgotten breaths.
They say the Gods were wicked slaves for
Righteous men to explain away their wrong-
Doings and hateful speech but Iodine words
Taste so sweet/ They say the Gods were wrathful
Things, titans of anger and beaten grief, rage
Directed at their thieves/ Human men who stole
Their game, the meat of honey dripping flames.
They say the Gods will never lie again, their
Days of Iodine speech forever ingrained in the
minds
Of many and the feet of few/ They say the Gods
Smell of chemical spills and rotten pills.

Sulfur

My sulfur devil rests on my shoulders where
God left a small birthmark in the shape of the
moon/ She cackles and dips her toes into the
Pool of burnt flesh, for holy hands cannot touch
Mortal sin without inflicting some kind of
Punishment/ I think she likes to feel the
remnants
Of my God's holy touch, I think she likes to
Defile it; playing with the strings of power like
A cat told not to knock that cup off the table.
When I tell her it's time to sleep, time to leave
That God alone, she laughs and exhales smoke.
Leaving sparks of ember along my skin/ She
Taps my birthmark, the one marked with sin, and
Asks me over and over again,
        "Do you think that God deserves such
peace?"
And I tell her, "No, but it's not my place to take
revenge."
And that sulfur devil asks again,
        "Then who will raise the final stake and
plunge it into holy flesh?"
Sometimes I think that little devil knows too
Much to share, and sometimes I think that
Maybe the smell of sulfur is the smell

Of holy flares.

Bleach

Sometimes the pain
Is so dull that I would
Prefer to feeling anything
Over nothing at all.
The only time I feel
Alive is when I drink
And cry and sip on that
Cracked cup of gasoline
And bleach/ The blood
That drips from my poor
Teeth only serves to
Remind me of how
Little I feel, and how
Much I wish to kill.
Afterall, bleach littered
Lungs and gasoline
Teeth feel much better
Than that dreaded
Eternal sleep.

Gasoline

Gasoline breathes with lungs like mine,
But hers are rotted with fungus and time.
Her bones have long since decayed, cities
Withering in her apocalyptic gaze/ I don't
Know what to do, she's ever present,
All-knowing and she's remembering my dues.
She talks like a rusted train, wheels turning
Within that wicked brain/ Gasoline smiles
Ignite dangerously without any plights
And she knows that I can never take flight.
My wings have rotted and grown stiff,
Knotted are my veins, a jumble of
Overgrown pain/ With each step I
Take towards the city limits, I feel
Her laughter echoing in my feet,
Pulling me back towards her undead fleet.
Gasoline rivers of abandoned hope flow
Along the pedestrian slopes/ The land
Is contaminated, diseased beyond repair,
And all she can muster to do is laugh
And sing with that chemical stare.

Calcium

My mother says she has a calcium baby,
That it grows and kicks within her womb;
But I don't trust her that easily, nor do I
Want to submit to that gloom/ She said I'd
Be her only child, one of flesh and blood,
But here she goes again, singing, that wretched
Boney song:
>"I have a son a'comin' to me,
>>And he ain't gonna be shrew,
>>He's gonna feel that steady
>>Solid touch, of those worn
>>Down calcium blues."

My mother says she has a calcium baby,
A son of hard shown work and honeydew,
But I don't love that easily, and I don't
Plan to dig my own tomb/ She said I'd be
A great big sister, a torch blinding the light,
But I can't help but sing my wet song, despite
All the calcium delights:
>"My body ain't a temple,
>>And it sure as hell ain't my

debut,
>>But I don't care and here I say
>>I'll never drink that glass 'o
>>Mildew."

My mother says she misses her calcium boy,
Her second child that she hew'd, but I don't
really
Believe her, and neither should you/ She always
Said she wanted a boy, one with those strong
sliver
Bones, but he didn't stop crying—those sharp
boney
Groans:
      "My mother ain't a saint and my father
        Got the blues, my sister knows a
thing
        And she let me get skewed/ My
calcium
        Bones ain't fit enough, God put
them in
Loosely screwed, but there is one thing I'm
Good for: the ol' family stew."
My mother says she has a calcium baby in her
Battered womb, but I don't trust her that easily,
And I don't wish for it to be true/ She's eaten her
Fill, God knows that to be the truth; and she's
shoved
Her wicked baby brew down my throat before I
could
Muster up the courage to chew.

Ammonia

Her name was Ammonia and she hailed
From the little European country of
Estonia/ She always talked a little
Strangely, and I never could fully
Understand; what could she mean when
She mumbled,
        "There be Gods helpin' hand."
Poor Ammonia always loved philosophical
debates,
Ending each paragraph with wholesome little
dates.
She said she liked to keep track of what, who,
where,
And when; what people said, and when they'd
say such
Silly things again.
December 12th, 1984, I told her I hated God and
much
Preferred death over his stupid holy wars/ It was
then she
Scribbled my words down, and looked me in the
eyes,
Asking me with such conviction,
        "Have you ever seen God cry?"

I told her with a laugh that I didn't believe in
such things,
And that God would fall before the feet of
mortal bloody kings.
She shook her head and tapped her pen along her
desk,
            "How can you say something so utterly
grotesque?"
I apologized and said,
            "My little Ammonia, dear, I forget
sometimes that my
                        Words do not adhere to your
way of thinking,
                        Your devoted religious ear."
            "Things like that are natural,"
She said,
            "Do not apologize, for I will never hear
your words
                        And condemn them with a
sneer."
My poor little Ammonia, she believed in God so
perfectly,
Never knowing he was near/ She thought he
rested in the skies,
And that's where she traveled to visit him that
September night,
But I'm sure she now knows that God sleeps not
in some holy land,
But under healthy human tears.

Cyanide

I always thought that I was
Breathless around you because
I loved you so, but it ends up
That was never true at all. Clyde,
Sure, I love you, but man, you
Had some secrets/ Why did you
Never tell me that you were dyed
In a pit of bubbling cyanide? I feel
Like that's something a wife should
Know, although I guess I would have
Left you sooner If I had known/ So I
Can't really blame you, but granted, you
Were slowly killing me so—I hope you
Feel some shame, you've ruined the
Family name/ Anyways, Clyde, you're
A really good guy, but I don't like my men
Dipped in abnormal amounts of Cyanide.
You'll find a chemical woman someday,
You just might have to pray or maybe,
Be gay?

Helium

I carry my love around like a balloon,
And everyone's always worried that it'll
Pop, but I have a secret, and it's that my
Mortal love will never stop/ My first balloon
Exploded, rubber streaming everywhere, my
Second one was mauled by a great big grizzly
Bear/ My third one I destroyed myself, in a fit
Of rage may I add, but that's okay because I
Did it on a great big stage besides a rocket
launching pad/ My mother said I'd run outta
Love soon, that one little girl can't make the
Whole world swoon, but I have secret that no
One really knows/ My balloon isn't made of
love
But lonesome Helium prose/ My love will never
Stop, because it never existed in the first place,
So that balloon can try and pop, but it will
always
Be replaced/ I carry my love around like a
balloon,
And by that, I mean it's a normal helium
balloon, but
Everyone in town will still peer at me and think
"what

An abnormal little child" And to that I will
surely drink.

Titanium

Titanium arms have never felt so sweet,
Wrapping around me like with a soul-like
Heat/ The metal creaks and groans, anything
But discrete, as the planets trace along my
Cobbled heartbeat/ My arms, on the contrary,
Are flesh and bones, loving titanium's hateful
Foe/ Luckily for me, the metal seems not to
Mind my dewberry touch—snapping limbs that
Ache and clutch/ My fragile mortal waist, the
Place where the heavens touch/ Despite the
Pain, the coldness, and the strangeness too,
I admire the dark blue hue/ Reminds me of
oceans
Past, the nightly skies, and the universe vast.
    "How did you come across a being so
outcast?"
—is what many of you may say, and to that
I raise the answer,
    "Why, the archway between the stars
and the moon,
        Where the Gods descend to go
and prune their
        Mighty gardens of fine-tuned
wishes, where

   Human men are not fed but the
feed for the
   Divine's dishes."
Titanium embraces that go against all
Natural laws, metal teeth grinding into
Nice blue jaws/ I do not care what others
Say, whatever hate and prejudice they
May spray; the only thing I care about
Is the fact that my titanium Goddess
Might have unloyal doubts.

Rose Oxide

Pink tipped honey hues, draped with lonely,
Artificial rules; laws that only beasts created
To heard their little sheep into their awaiting
jaws/ They say their cause is for the masses,
But good women die while bad men brandish
their
Opera glasses, sitting in their capitalist pews,
Refusing to adopt a humane and kind view.
These beasts say that "life is unfair" that
The world doesn't care, that Mother Earth
Only gave to birth to such creatures as I in
Order to prove corrupted men's worth/ But
I see through the rose glittered glass that these
Unruly men composed; I see what they want me
To think, want me to be: someone who will
never
Oppose, a woman who will give birth to a
healthy
Human son/ To this I object, to this I shatter the
rose
Petals in my lungs/ For these beasts shall never
outrun
My passion and drive to change what it means to
be

alive/ I will thrive under the shouts and screams
of
Angered men, knowing that they will never be
able
To put me back in my mental pen—that they
cannot
Control what I think! For I have seen the world
in both
Their wicked pink and the people's written ink!
They
Can carve rose colored glass out of their
blood-crafted brass
And shove it down my sass filled throat, but I
will
Ensure that they can never gloat/ For the people
wrote
About their sins and will forever note the pain
that
We suffered under their steel-toed votes.

Alcian Blue

I don't have a God. I realized this when
I was laying in the light blue of my bathrooms
Leaky faucet water. The lights weren't on,
That was a conscious decision, I designed the
Mood that way. Instead, I brought a small little
Lamp and set it on the floor next to my phone,
Where old music played distantly like when you
Try and think about home. The darkness
somehow
Made the water feel lighter, like it's problems
Had melted away—the low thrum of echoing
music
Took my mind off my own. My shadow danced
Along the walls and put on a little show. As I
watched
My fake body sway to the lonely music I had put
on,
I realized that there was no God, and that I,
alone,
Am divine. I realized flesh is natural and nothing
to
Be ashamed off—the curve of my legs forged by
My younger years roughing around in the late
winter

Snow, my slim fingers the product of all the
words I
Carefully carved and nicked. The valley of my
breasts
Nothing more but another addition to this
evolution
And adaptation of my human body, the one I
currently call
Home. I realized that most problems I face are
all creations
Of humanities folly, some problems even birthed
from my
Own stupidity. I thought about the evil of people
and consequently
Thought about the irony of it all. We are not evil,
we were not
Born that way but made. And we are not good,
we were not born
As saviors and Gods but forged that path on our
own.
Others may have a God, one that they look to for
guidance, or
Other mortal quirks, but I've never had one of
those, and I'm glad
I never did. The leaky faucet blue of my
bathroom cracked tub
Is the closest thing to a God that I've ever
stumbled upon.

My religious experience was not in a church or
pew, but alone
Sinking into my bathrooms Alcian blue.

Mercury

My mother always gave me Mercury spoons
To wrap my tongue around when my fingers
Began to prune/ It wasn't good for a young child
Like I, to be defiled by the sickness that was
birthed
From the skies/ I was a child of the ground; of
Earth, dirt,
And mirth; clouds, rain, and the suns girth were
not meant
For me, but the birds/ My mother always said
that Mercury
Had the cure; It'd wipe those silly flying
thoughts from my mind—
She fully assured/ For her, and her worries, I
endured but
Oftentimes I'd think that perhaps there was a
missing link
Within my Earthly life—how would it feel to
fly?
Soar up into the heavenly skies, to never again
Comply to Mercury drinks but to be free oh so
beastly!
Wings of wild rye and little sparrows battle
cries; they'd

Sit upon my awaiting back, loyal to me like a
forest's
Wolf pack/ But those dreams are far from reality,
my spirit
Churning like Mother's black tea/ For now I'll
settle to forget,
Waking up each night in a sky like cold sweat.

Nicotine

He laced the air with red stained heat, the
wicked
Rusty dust settling within my bones/ It made my
Lungs shake and quiver, blood swirling into one
Massive metal-flavored river—but when I raised
My ink-filled concerns, he said that there was
Nothing he could do/ The damage had already
Been done/ But three days later, as the doctors
Poured over me like a crimson tsunami, he
Appeared with that sly smile and said to me,
      "I found a cure, somethin' good.
          It'll make those melting lungs
          Go back to how they should."
I accepted the cup of Nicotine lies, pouring that
Tinted gray over my surgery withered eyes/ Of
Course I knew that this might be a ploy, but the
Pain in my chest could no longer be ignored.
Three weeks later I'm coughing up a storm,
throat
Dyed red with busted blood veins and more/ I
called
Him over and asked for help—he shook his head
and
Said once more,
      "There's nothing I can do,

The damage has been done."
But this time he raised a white-gloved hand and
Revealed a palm of red dusty pills, tilting his
head
Back as his body shook with thrill/ He parted his
orange
Cracked lips and bellowed out,
          "Since we're friends, you and I,
                    I'll lower the price of this handy
                    Life-saving dye/ It'll cure those
Nicotine
                    Ash flavored cries!"
          "You're the one who cursed me so!
                    First dispersed that hell-ish
plague!
                    And now that I am at my worst,
you
                    Dive in headfirst? You coerced,
played
                    A twisted verse, made me suffer
from
                    Addictive thirst!"
He shrugged and twirled the pills in his dainty
hands,
          "We all have to make a profit,
                    So, I did what saw fit."
          "You poisoned me for a moment's fun?
                    A single penny for my life, and
now

You're done?"
"You would've done the same, hun'."

Sodium

Sodium toes are hard to walk with.
Those weak bones and salty little
hormones/ My feet always bend
And tend to sway to the tide of
Rocking shipsides/ The sailors
Of the bay say that it's a blessed
Guide—that Sodium toes will
Show me to where the solemn
Water flows/ But when I trip
On my salt-froze toes, I think
That the men of the seas only
Speak in ancient, outdated
prose/ Sodium bones and low
Ocean tones are nothing but
Dead Gods moans.

Uranium

I think I'd like to
See that green again—
                    "The toxic one?"
          Yes.
                              "Why?"
Something just felt like home. I can't help but
think
          Of my mother's old comb.
"The one your father carved
               From starved wooden stars?"
                         Yes, that's the one! The
comb that seemed to
          Capture the
                    Rising sun.
                              "It was
pretty—I will admit,
          But are you willing to risk
Your wit and challenge the Gods to quit?"
I am. So what of it?
                         "Nothing. Except that
Uranium green happened
               To slit the neck of
                         Your lover and
          Friends.
So why risk it all

Again?"
Because the human soul
Is a strange thing to behold.

It can never be controlled.

Carbon

"Why are you here?"
Why do you care?
"Because you're something to fear."
Are you going to say a prayer?
"You don't sound sincere."
Because your God only ensnares.
"Nay, you do—with that wicked sneer."
Don't forget my withering glare.
"You dare to mock and jeer!"
What? Are you scared?
"No! For I have God's mighty spear."
Oh, what a divine and holy flair.
"I will ask again, why do you appear?"
Maybe to tell you to beware.
"You threaten a holy man? Disappear!"
My, my—you're full of hot air.
"Go! Or the punishment will be severe."
Do you think an unbeliever fears the Lord's
prayer?
"I will rip off your sinful ear!"
Go ahead and try. You will get nowhere.
"Prepare! For your soul shall now be sheared!"
Oh—should I be scared? A human of pompous
folly dares to

Bare their flatted teeth at the wreath of truth and
hate? Their
Stupidity must surely be great. Before me now
you lay, cracked breastplate
And instincts of that of a primate. You are made
from carbon and stardust, I
From space, truth, and wanderlust. You speak of
a God long dead, and twist
His words into that of pure dread. Here the devil
is not I, but you. The instigator of sin and the
corrupter of truth.

Charcoal

I burned like charcoal, body intact and whole.
Dying so young was not my goal but life is
Anything but an easy stroll/ If anything it's like
If a black hole had married a soul and produced
An heir akin to a divine troll/ Though what can I
Say? I'm human and dull, playing a
predetermined
Universal role! There was no control for me, that
Was fake/ And sadly I could never find that
immortal
Loophole/ Anyways, this poem is nothing but a
Pinhole in the fabric of time and space, but hey!
Would you rather have nothing or an atom-sized
Porthole? I think the answer is clear and that's
all I
Have to say about this life-sized sinkhole/ Oh
wait,
One last thing to let you know! Keep in mind
that life
Itself will never have a public opinion poll.

* 9 7 8 9 3 5 7 2 1 5 1 8 3 *